MODAL HANON

50 Exercises for the Intermediate to Advanced Pianist

by Peter Deneff

ISBN 978-1-5400-2272-1

Visit Hal Leonard Online at
www.halleonard.com

Contact Us:
Hal Leonard
7777 West Bluemound Road
Milwaukee, WI 53213
Email: info@halleonard.com

In Europe contact:
Hal Leonard Europe Limited
42 Wigmore Street
Marylebone, London, W1U 2RN
Email: info@halleonardeurope.com

In Australia contact:
Hal Leonard Australia Pty. Ltd.
4 Lentara Court
Cheltenham, Victoria, 3192 Australia
Email: info@halleonard.com.au

Acknowledgements

I would like to thank all the people in my life who have encouraged and supported me in my musical journey. My parents, George V. Deneff and Alkisti Deneff, my children, Gitana, George, and Sophia, and most of all, my wife, Diane, who continues to inspire, encourage and support me in my life and career. Lastly, I would like to thank all of the musicians and fans who continue to support me through my performances, recordings, and of course, enjoying my books!

About the author

Peter Deneff grew up in a musical home, exposed to classical music, Greek songs, and the Beatles. After several years of classical piano lessons with Leaine Gibson, he began jazz studies with the world-renowned pianist and David Bowie band member, Mike Garson. During this time he also studied many ethnic styles that influenced his composition and playing. He studied music composition and film scoring at California State University Long Beach, where he earned his bachelor's and master's degrees in classical music composition. While at CSULB, Deneff composed his *Three Greek Dances for String Quartet*, which has been performed in the U.S., Canada, and Australia.

Peter has written many best-selling books for Hal Leonard Corporation and has produced and recorded numerous arrangements for Yamaha, Hal Leonard, and PianoDisc. His original music and scoring was featured in the award-winning Charlie Sheen film, *Five Aces*. In 2012, Deneff composed the score for the feature film *Love of Life*. In early 2013, his involvement with the Hollywood animation community afforded him the opportunity to write the score for the short film, "The Annies: 40 Year Retrospective" which was presented as one of the highlights of the 2013 Annie Awards at Royce Hall, UCLA, and featured the legendary voice actress June Foray. Also, in 2013, Deneff scored the film, *A Journey into the Holocaust*, produced by Paul Bachow.

His stylistic versatility on the keyboard has allowed him to perform with a diverse assortment of artists such as Tierra, Ike Willis (Frank Zappa), Ramon Banda, Jerry Salas (El Chicano), Chalo Eduardo as well as jazz greats, Robert Kyle, Bruce Babad, Bijon Watson, and Tom Brechtlein. Deneff has also performed and directed numerous international recording artists like Sonia Santos, Rita Sakellariou, Giorgos Margaritis, Stathis Aggelopoulos, Vatche, Shimi Tavori, and Persian international superstar Ebi.

Deneff's original project, Excursion, features mostly original works in a style that could be best described as *ethno-jazz*. Excursion's sound is a blend of Brazilian, Cuban, Greek, Armenian, classical, and progressive jazz. The group has been featured twice at the Playboy Jazz Festival and regularly performs at Herb Alpert's Vibrato Jazz Grill and at the World Famous Baked Potato in Hollywood.

On the academic side, Peter has taught at Musician's Institute Hollywood, Orange County High School of the Arts, Cypress College, and Fullerton College.

Introduction

Practically all piano students are familiar with the study of scales. They are an inextricable part of piano pedagogy and, of course, an elemental building block of music. However, most students do not have much experience playing scales beyond the familiar seven-note sets on which western music is built: the major scale and the three "flavors" of minor. This doesn't inherently present a problem as long as the pianist is studying predominantly classical music from the Baroque through the Romantic era. But it can be quite limiting if one is exploring the varied melodic sound worlds of jazz, world music, pop, and even modern concert and film music. The seemingly endless variety of non-western scales is a deep well of musical material which can be an essential tool for the pianist, composer or improviser.

Modal Hanon is a valuable introduction to the world of alternative scales. While it is not intended to be an exhaustive codex of all non-western scales (that would take endless volumes), it is a practical introduction to some of the most common modes that composers and improvisers employ. It is not only a lesson in the learning of scales, it is also another vehicle for building one's technique and "chops" through the use of non-western patterns. They are like a foreign language for the hands! These etudes will train your fingers to play melodic patterns that are unfamiliar to them. I have also made sure to include atypical meters to add an interesting rhythmic element to them. They will open up your ears and imagination as you become familiar with their sound. In addition to the exercises, I have included an Index of Scales which can be used as a reference for practicing the scales and can help familiarize the student with their sound and character before studying the corresponding exercise.

Here are some suggestions that will help maximize your results:
- Start slowly and don't practice any exercise faster than you can accurately play it.
- Always use a metronome.
- Keep your fingers curved, hands low, and play on your fingertips.
- Observe the recommended fingerings.
- Maintain good posture, stay relaxed, and breathe!
- Memorize the exercises and internalize the patterns.
- Practice them in twelve keys.
- Be creative with them, compose variations, and most importantly…have fun!

I hope that this volume will become a staple of your practice regimen. The exercises are intended to help you explore uncharted melodic sound-worlds. They are fun to play, while still providing a challenging approach to technique practice. No matter how you decide to employ these etudes, they are sure to provide an enjoyable and satisfying approach to developing your chops and finger strength.

Happy practicing!

Peter Deneff

Contents

Exercise	Page	Exercise	Page
1. Dorian	6	27. Sabah	82
2. Dorian	9	28. Sabah	84
3. Dorian	12	29. Huzzam	86
4. Phrygian	15	30. Huzzam	88
5. Phrygian	18	31. Purvi Theta	93
6. Phrygian	21	32. Purvi Theta	96
7. Aeolian	24	33. Romanian Minor	98
8. Aeolian	27	34. Romanian Minor	100
9. Aeolian	30	35. Romanian Minor	104
10. Mixolydian	32	36. Hungarian Minor	107
11. Mixolydian	34	37. Hungarian Minor	112
12. Lydian	36	38. Hungarian Minor	114
13. Lydian	38	39. Hungarian Gypsy	116
14. Locrian	41	40. Hungarian Gypsy	119
15. Locrian	44	41. Hungarian Gypsy	122
16. Super Locrian	47	42. Raga None	129
17. Super Locrian	50	43. Japanese (In Sen)	132
18. Hijaz	52	44. Japanese (In Sen)	134
19. Hijaz	58	45. Hirajoshi	136
20. Hijaz	62	46. Hirajoshi	138
21. Byzantine	65	47. Balinese Pelog	140
22. Byzantine	66	48. Balinese Pelog	143
23. Byzantine	68	49. Neapolitan Minor	144
24. Kiourdi	73	50. Neapolitan Minor	146
25. Kiourdi	76		
26. Kiourdi	79	Index of Scales	148

1
Dorian

8va -

(8va) -

8va -

2
Dorian

11

3
Dorian

4
Phrygian

5
Phrygian

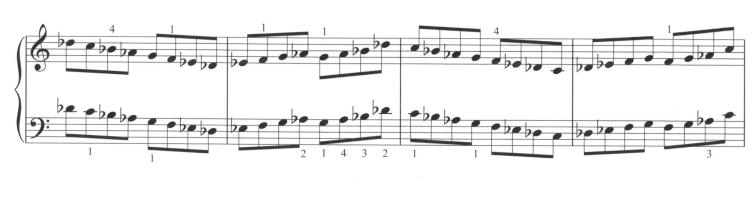

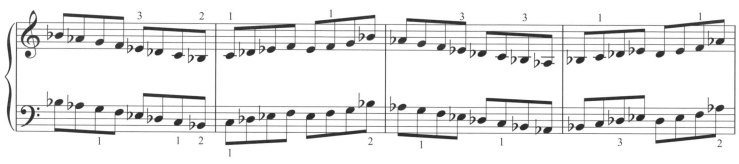

6
Phrygian

7
Aeolian

8
Aeolian

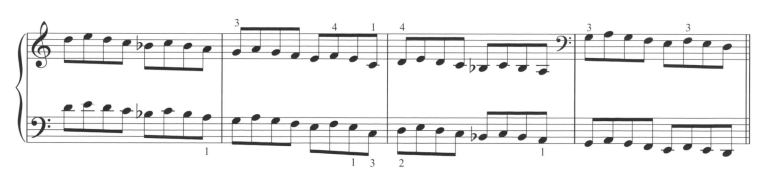

9
Aeolian

10
Mixolydian

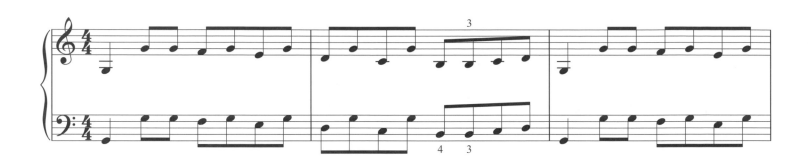

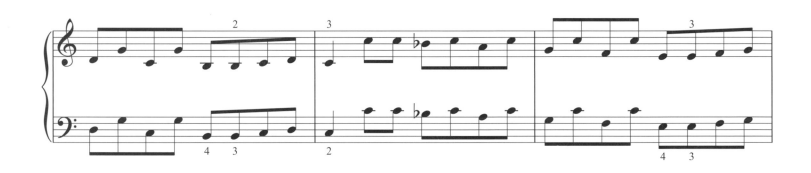

11
Mixolydian

12
Lydian

13
Lydian

14
Locrian

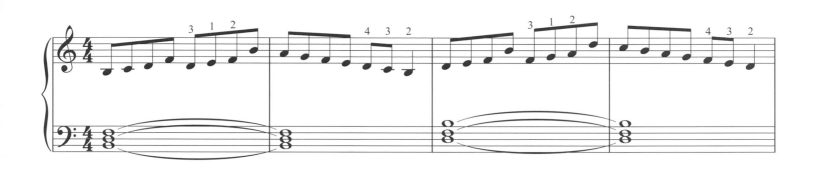

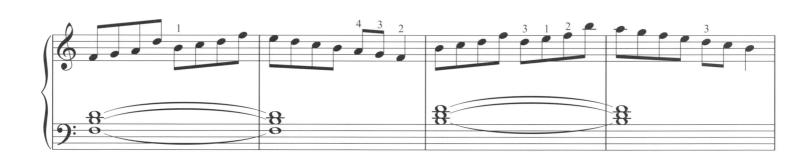

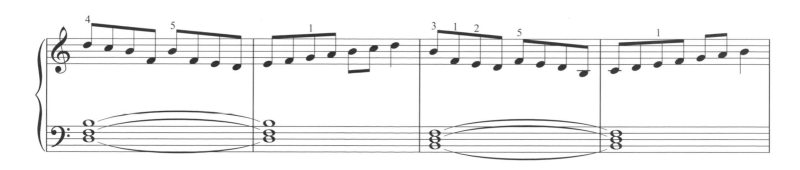

15
Locrian

16
Super Locrian

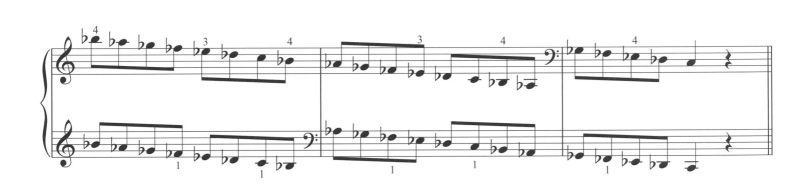

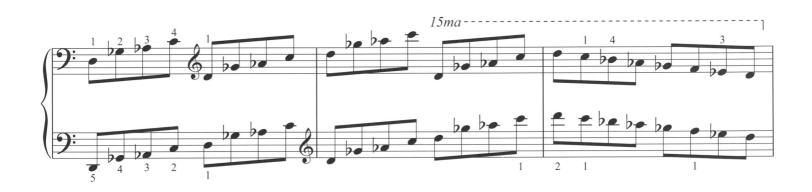

17
Super Locrian

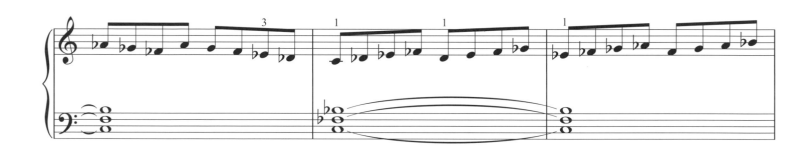

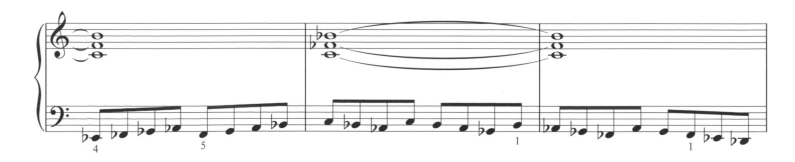

18
Hijaz

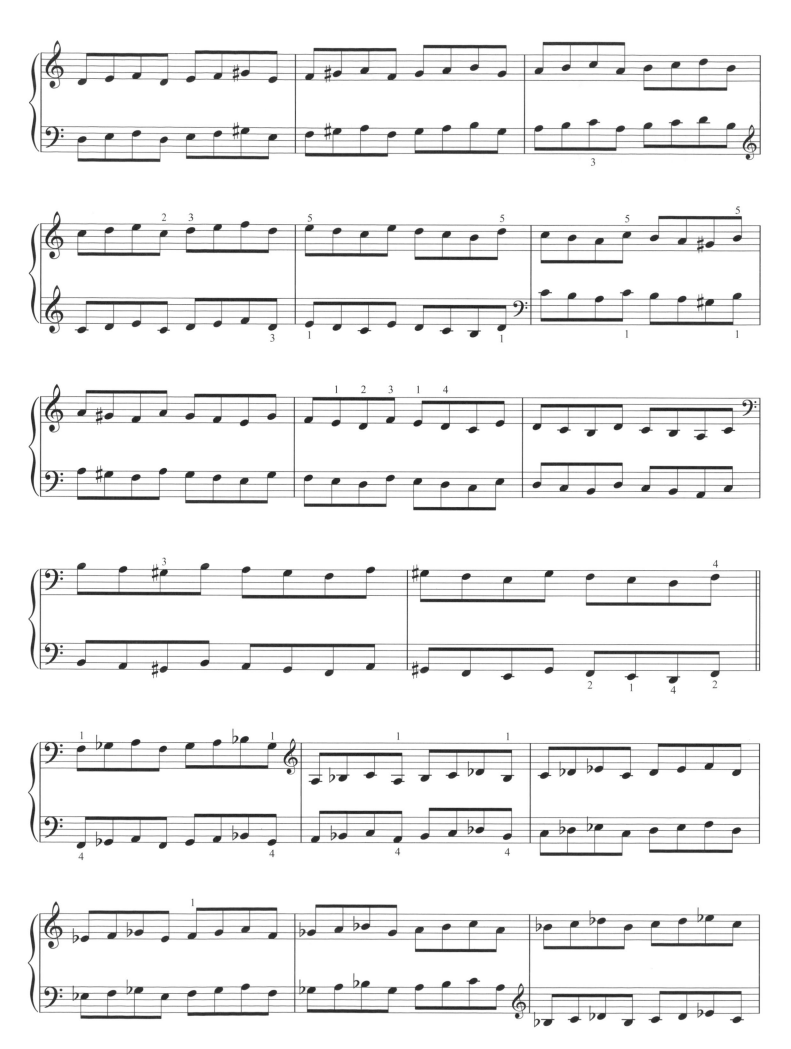

19
Hijaz

20
Hijaz

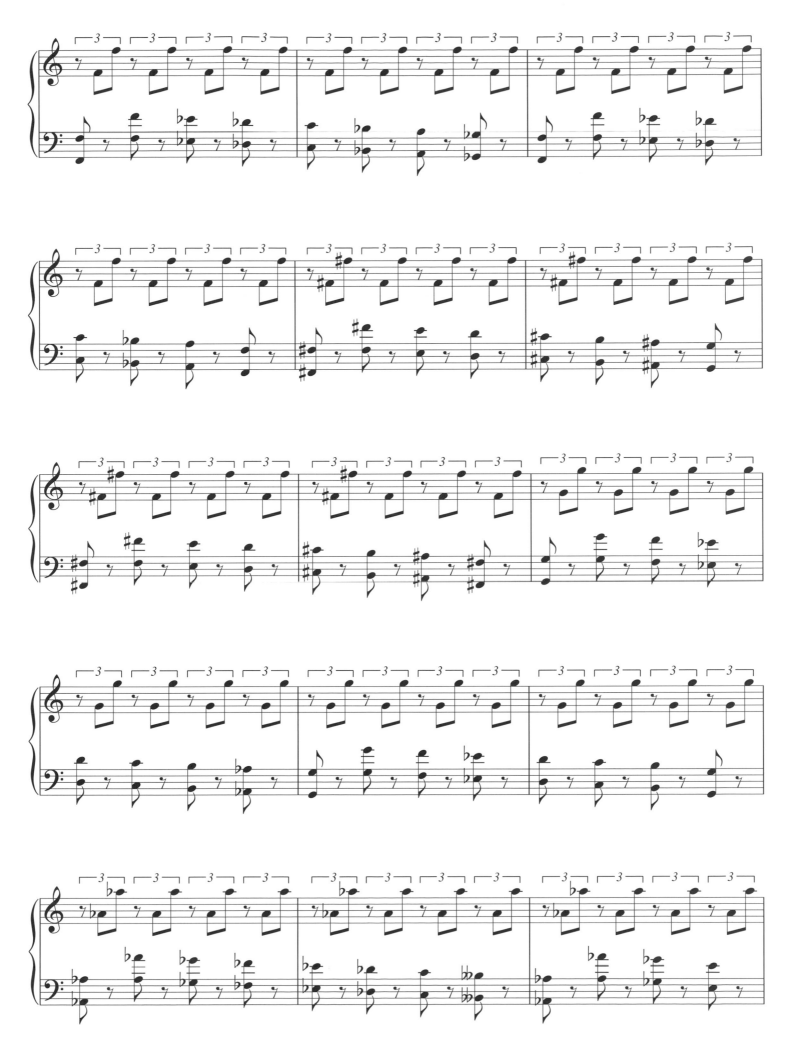

21
Byzantine

22
Byzantine

23
Byzantine

70

24
Kiourdi

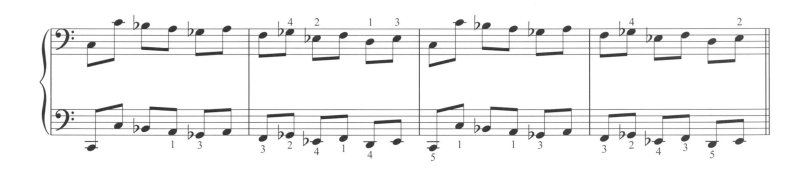

25
Kiourdi

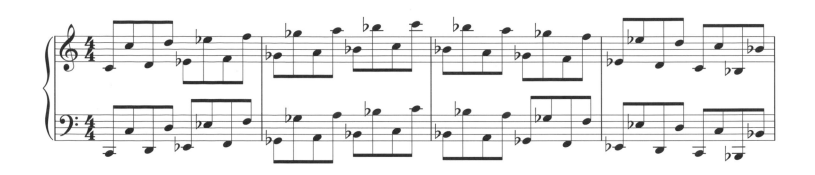

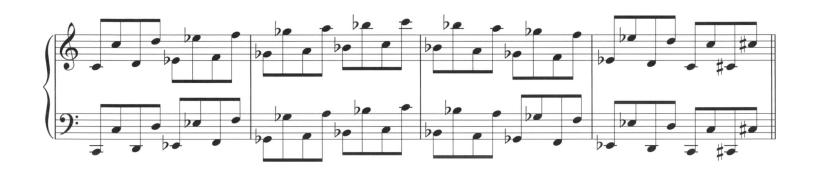

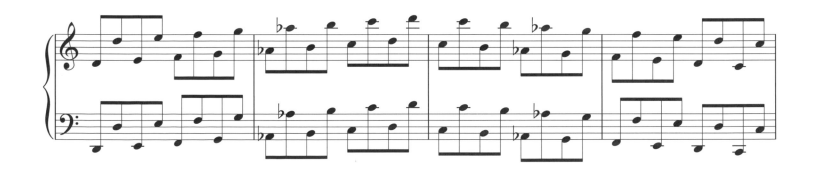

26
Kiourdi

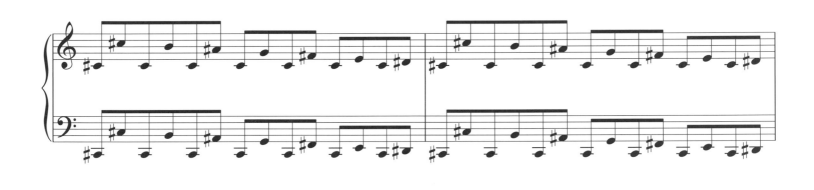

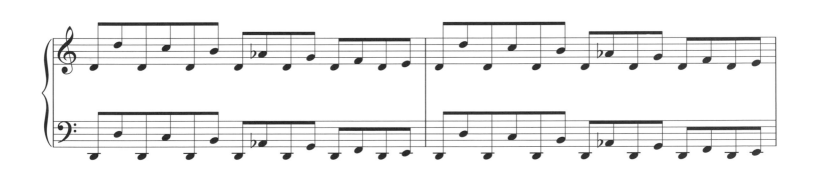

27
Sabah

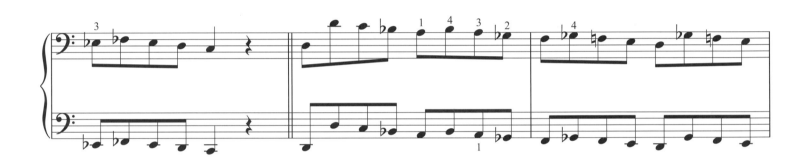

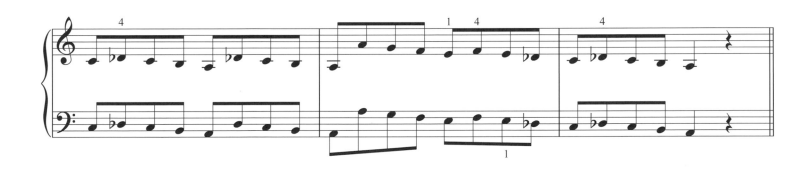

28
Sabah

29
Huzzam

30
Huzzam

89

31
Purvi Theta

32
Purvi Theta

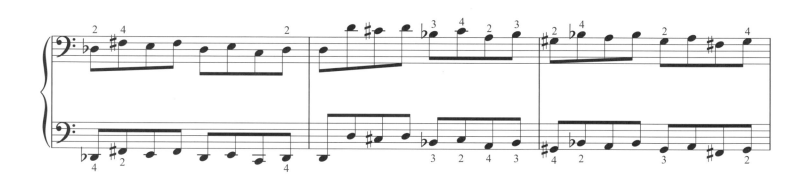

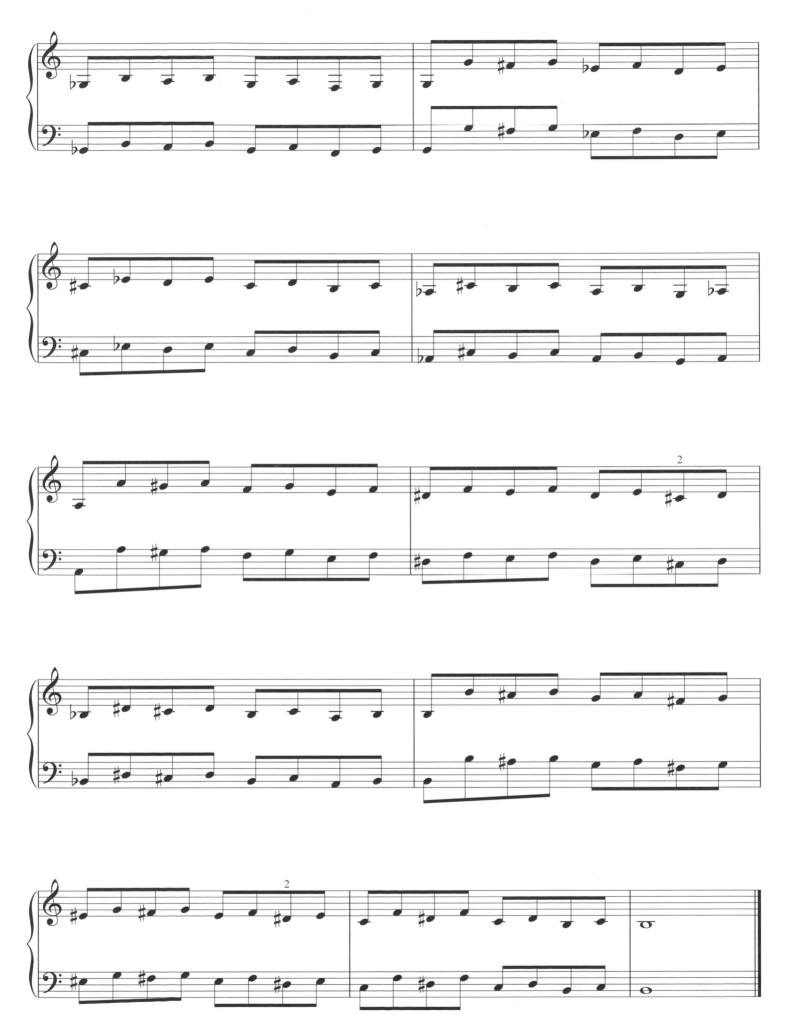

33
Romanian Minor

34
Romanian Minor

35
Romanian Minor

105

36
Hungarian Minor

108

37
Hungarian Minor

38
Hungarian Minor

115

39
Hungarian Gypsy

40
Hungarian Gypsy

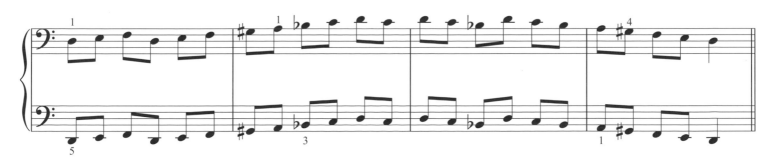

41
Hungarian Gypsy

42
Raga None

130

43
Japanese (In Sen)

44
Japanese (In Sen)

45
Hirajoshi

46
Hirajoshi

47
Balinese Pelog

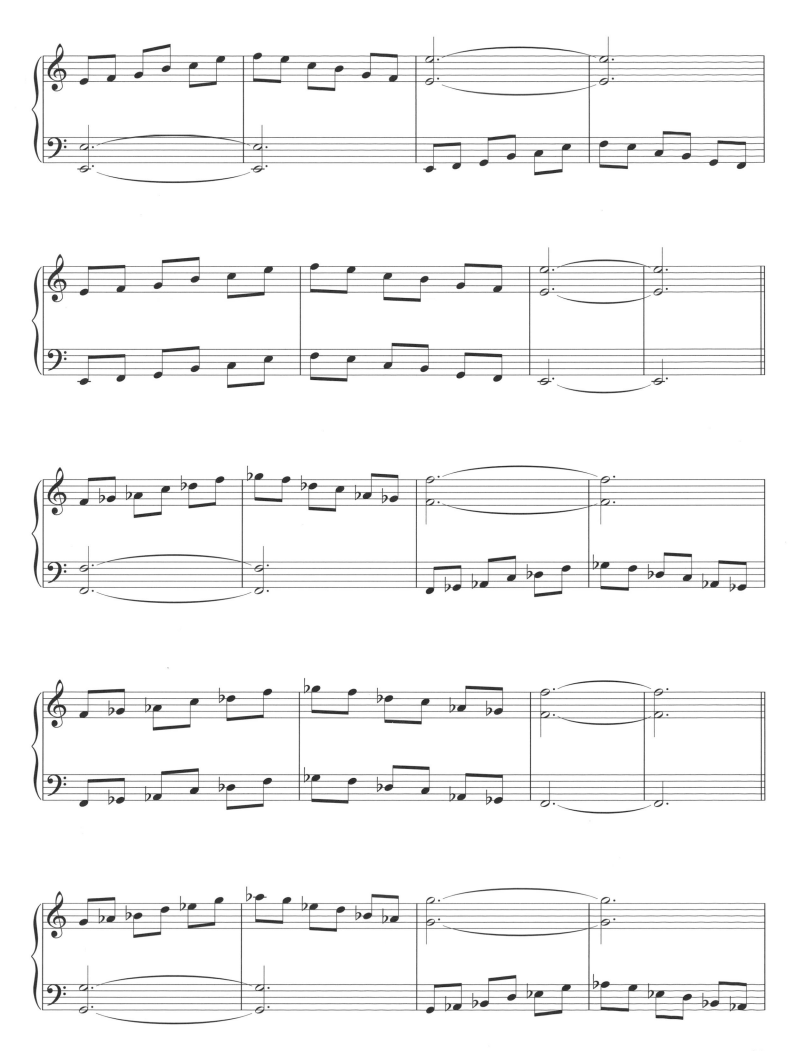

48
Balinese Pelog

49
Neapolitan Minor

145

50
Neapolitan Minor

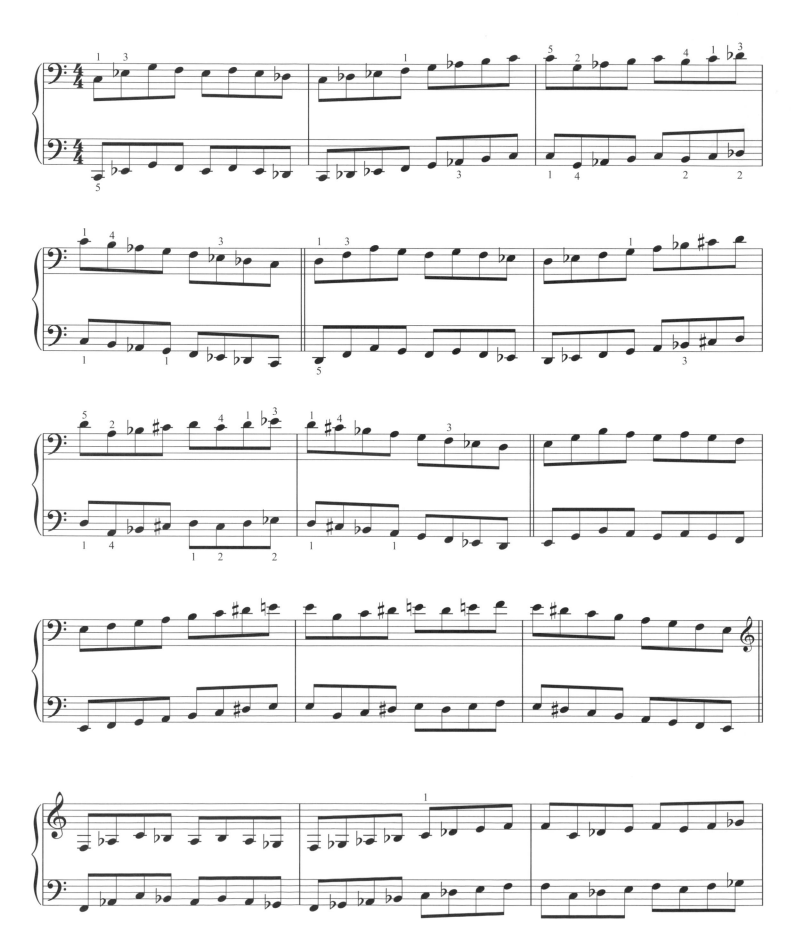

Index of Scales
(With C Root)

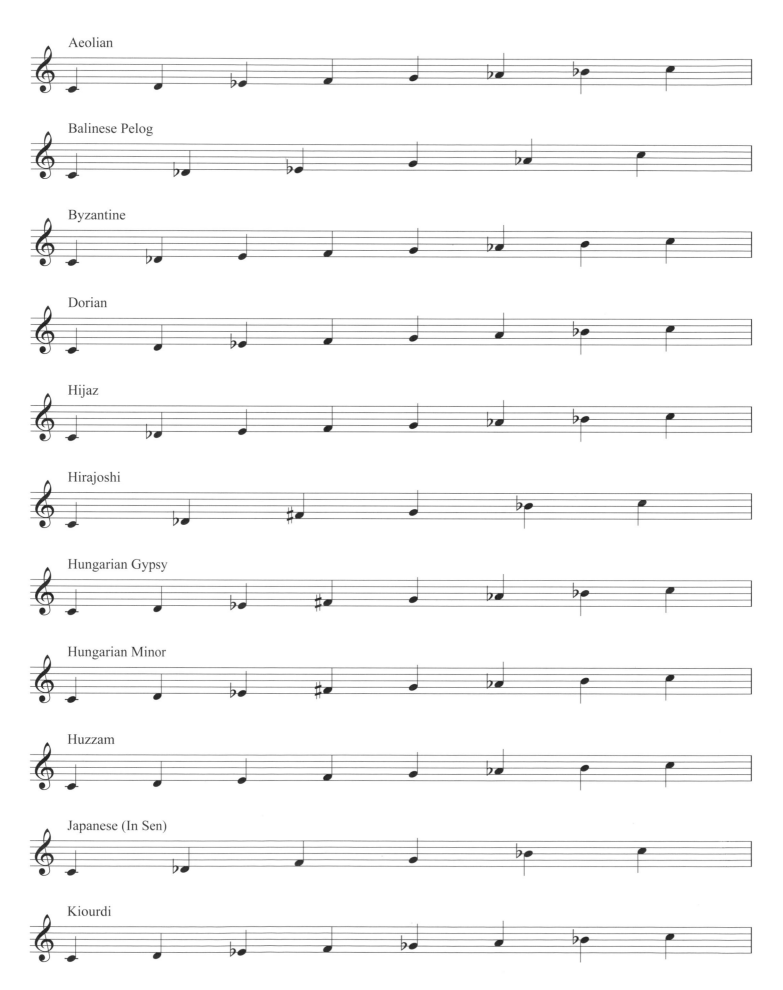

MUSICIANS INSTITUTE ™

Musicians Institute Press is the official series of instructional publications from Southern California's renowned music school, Musicians Institute. These books, book/audio packages, and videos have been created by MI instructors who are among the world's best and most experienced professional musicians.

KEYBOARD

00695708	Blues Hanon by Peter Deneff	$17.99
00695556	Dictionary of Keyboard Grooves by Gail Johnson – Book/CD	$16.95
00202430	Easy Jazz Hanon by Peter Deneff – Book/Audio	$12.99
00695336	Funk Keyboards – The Complete Method by Gail Johnson – Book/Audio	$16.99
00695936	Hip-Hop Keyboard by Henry Soleh Brewer – Book/CD	$17.95
00695791	Jazz Chord Hanon by Peter Deneff	$17.99
00695554	Jazz Hanon by Peter Deneff	$16.99
00695773	Jazz Piano by Christian Klikovits – Book/CD	$19.99
00695209	Keyboard Voicings by Kevin King	$12.95
00266448	Modal Hanon by Peter Deneff	$14.99
00145419	Pop Keyboard Concepts by Christian Klikovits – Book/Audio	$19.99
00695509	Pop Rock Keyboards by Henry Sol-Eh Brewer & David Garfield – Book/CD	$19.95
00695784	Rock Hanon by Peter Deneff	$19.99
00695226	Salsa Hanon by Peter Deneff	$17.99
00695939	Samba Hanon by Peter Deneff	$16.99
00695882	Stride Hanon by Peter Deneff	$17.99

VOICE

00695883	Advanced Vocal Technique by Dena Murray and Tita Hutchison – Book/Audio	$19.99
00695262	Harmony Vocals by Mike Campbell & Tracee Lewis – Book/Audio	$19.99
00695626	The Musician's Guide to Recording Vocals by Dallan Beck – Book/CD	$15.99
00695629	Rock Vocals by Coreen Sheehan – Book/CD	$17.99
00695195	Sightsinging by Mike Campbell	$19.99
00695427	Vocal Technique by Dena Murray – Book/Audio	$24.99

GUITAR

00695922	Acoustic Artistry by Evan Hirschelman – Book/Audio	$19.99
00695298	Advanced Scale Concepts and Licks for Guitar by Jean Marc Belkadi – Book/CD	$17.99
00217709	All-in-One Guitar Soloing Course by Daniel Gilbert & Beth Marlis	$29.99
00695132	Blues Guitar Soloing by Keith Wyatt – Book/Online Media	$24.99
00695680	Blues/Rock Soloing for Guitar by Robert Calva – Book/Audio	$19.99
00695131	Blues Rhythm Guitar by Keith Wyatt – Book/Audio	$19.99
00696002	Modern Techniques for the Electric Guitarist by Dean Brown – DVD	$29.95
00695664	Chord Progressions for Guitar by Tom Kolb – Book/CD	$17.99
00695855	Chord Tone Soloing by Barrett Tagliarino – Book/Audio	$24.99
00695646	Chord-Melody Guitar by Bruce Buckingham – Book/CD	$19.99
00695171	Classical & Fingerstyle Guitar Techniques by David Oakes – Book/Audio	$17.99
00695806	Classical Themes for Electric Guitar by Jean Marc Belkadi – Book/CD	$15.99
00695661	Country Guitar by Al Bonhomme – Book/Audio	$19.99

00695227	The Diminished Scale for Guitar by Jean Marc Belkadi – Book/CD	$14.99
00695181	Essential Rhythm Guitar by Steve Trovato – Book/CD	$15.99
00695873	Ethnic Rhythms for Electric Guitar by Jean Marc Belkadi – Book/CD	$17.99
00695860	Exotic Scales & Licks for Electric Guitar by Jean Marc Belkadi – Book/CD	$16.95
00695419	Funk Guitar by Ross Bolton – Book/Audio	$15.99
00695134	Guitar Basics by Bruce Buckingham – Book/Audio	$17.99
00695712	Guitar Fretboard Workbook by Barrett Tagliarino	$19.99
00695321	Guitar Hanon by Peter Deneff	$14.99
00695482	The Guitar Lick•tionary by Dave Hill – Book/CD	$19.99
00695190	Guitar Soloing by Daniel Gilbert and Beth Marlis – Book/Audio	$22.99
00695169	Harmonics by Jamie Findlay – Book/CD	$13.99
00695406	Introduction to Jazz Guitar Soloing by Joe Elliott – Book/Audio	$19.95
00695291	Jazz Guitar Chord System by Scott Henderson	$12.99
00217711	Jazz Guitar Improvisation by Sid Jacobs – Book/Online Media	$19.99
00217690	Jazz, Rock & Funk Guitar by Dean Brown – Book/Online Media	$19.99
00695361	Jazz-Rock Triad Improvising for Guitar by Jean Marc Belkadi – Book/CD	$15.99
00695379	Latin Guitar by Bruce Buckingham – Book/Audio	$17.99
00696656	Liquid Legato by Allen Hinds – Book/CD	$14.99
00695143	A Modern Approach to Jazz, Rock & Fusion Guitar by Jean Marc Belkadi – Book/CD	$15.99
00695711	Modern Jazz Concepts for Guitar by Sid Jacobs – Book/CD	$16.95
00695682	Modern Rock Rhythm Guitar by Danny Gill – Book/CD	$16.95
00695555	Modes for Guitar by Tom Kolb – Book/Audio	$18.99
00695192	Music Reading for Guitar by David Oakes	$19.99
00695697	Outside Guitar Licks by Jean Marc Belkadi – Book/CD	$16.99
00695962	Power Plucking by Dale Turner – Book/CD	$19.95
00695748	Progressive Tapping Licks by Jean Marc Belkadi – Book/CD	$16.99
00114559	Rhythm Guitar by Bruce Buckingham & Eric Paschal – Book/Audio	$24.99
00695188	Rhythm Guitar by Bruce Buckingham & Eric Paschal – Book	$19.99
00695909	Rhythm Guitar featuring Bruce Buckingham – DVD	$19.95
00110263	Rhythmic Lead Guitar by Barrett Tagliarino – Book/Audio	$19.99
00695144	Rock Lead Basics by Nick Nolan and Danny Gill – Book/Audio	$18.99
00695278	Rock Lead Performance by Nick Nolan and Danny Gill – Book/Audio	$17.99
00695146	Rock Lead Techniques by Nick Nolan and Danny Gill – Book/Audio	$16.99
00695977	Shred Guitar by Greg Harrison – Book/Audio	$19.99
00139556	Solo Slap Guitar by Jude Gold – Book/Video	$19.99
00695645	Slap & Pop Technique for Guitar by Jean Marc Belkadi – Book/CD	$16.99
00695913	Technique Exercises for Guitar by Jean Marc Belkadi – Book/CD	$15.99
00695340	Texas Blues Guitar by Robert Calva – Book/Audio	$17.99
00695863	Ultimate Guitar Technique by Bill LaFleur – Book/Audio	$22.99